Let's Cook!

Japan

The Culture and Recipes of Japan

Tracey Kelly

PowerKiDS
press.

Published in 2017 by
The Rosen Publishing Group, Inc.
29 East 21st Street, New York, NY 10010

Cataloging-in-Publication Data
Names: Kelly, Tracey.
Title: Culture and recipes of Japan / Tracey Kelly.
Description: New York : PowerKids Press, 2017. | Series: Let's cook! | Includes index.
Identifiers: ISBN 9781499431834 (pbk.) | ISBN 9781499432633 (library bound) | ISBN 9781499431841 (6 pack)
Subjects: LCSH: Cooking, Japanese--Juvenile literature. | Food habits--Japan--Juvenile literature. | Japan--Social
    life and customs--Juvenile literature.
Classification: LCC TX724.5.J3 K455 2017 | DDC 641.5952--dc23

For Brown Bear Books Ltd:
Text and Editor: Tracey Kelly
Editorial Director: Lindsey Lowe
Children's Publisher: Anne O'Daly
Design Manager: Keith Davis
Designer: Melissa Roskell
Picture Manager: Sophie Mortimer

Picture Credits: t=top, c=center, b=bottom, l=left, r=right. Front Cover: Shutterstock: KPG_Payless c,
KAMONRAT r, taa22 r, LanaN l, Kongsak l, rook76 c, Noppasin t, milezaway t. Inside: 123rf: 38-39t, 41, Harris
Shiffman 35b; Dreamstime: 28-29b, Filip Fuxa 23tr; Shutterstock: 1, 5br, 6-7t, 8-9b, 9br, 11br, 21br, 22b, 28-29t,
30b, 36bl, 38-39b, Akiyoko 30r, 39, Prinn Chansingthong 36-37t, easycamera 5r, Juan Salmoral Franco 22t,
Attila Jandi 31br, Perati Komson 36-37c, KPG Payless 6bl, 20-21t, Ziggy Mars 29, R. Nagy 20-21b, Tupungato 10,
VectorLifestylepic 31t; Thinkstock: istockphoto 4l, 7b, 10-11t, 37bl, 45, Ziggy Mars 22-23b, Marcel Okrelling 19,
Sean Pavone 8-9t.

Special thanks to Klaus Arras for all other photography.

Manufactured in the United States of America
CPSIA Compliance Information: Batch #BW17PK: For Further Information contact Rosen Publishing, New York, New York at 1-800-237-9932.

Contents

Looking at Japan

ASIA

Japan

Japan is a fascinating country with many contrasts. Its culture is a mix of high-tech inventions and traditional customs. And its cuisine is both unique and delicious!

Japan is a country in East Asia made up of four large and thousands of small islands. Its neighbors are Russia, Korea, and China.

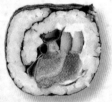

Long Live Japan!

Japan is a country made up of four main islands and thousands of small islands—6,852 altogether! If you put them together, their combined area would be about the size of California. Japan is a land of stunning natural landscapes. There are mountain ranges with towering peaks and twisting valleys, as well as lakes, rivers, and miles of coastline. Around 66 percent of the land area is covered with forests. In contrast, Japan's capital, Tokyo, is one of the busiest moderns cities in the world. It leads the world in the high-tech industry, but it also has some of the country's most ancient historical palaces and shrines. Japan's 127 million people all share one thing: a love of its fresh, healthy foods. Nippon Banzai (Long Live Japan)!

Rice and seaweed-wrapped sushi comes in many varieties. People around the world enjoy this Japanese dish.

Japan's mountains are home to breathtaking views and crater lakes, such as Okamo in the Zaõ Mountains, on Honshu Island.

CHINA

RUSSIA

SEA OF OKHOTSK

○ Sapporo
HOKKAIDO

SEA OF JAPAN

JAPAN

NORTH KOREA

The busy Akihabara area in Tokyo is home to the city's electronics shopping district.

SOUTH KOREA

HONSHU

○ **Tokyo**

○**Kyoto**
○**Kobe**
Hiroshima ○ ○**Osaka**
SHIKOKU
○ **Nagasaki**
KYUSHU

OSUMI ISLANDS

PACIFIC OCEAN

RYUKYU ISLANDS

AMAMI ISLANDS

OKINAWA ISLANDS

A tropical beach on Amami Oshima is one of many vacation spots in the Japanese Ryukyu Islands.

Honshu Island

Honshu, Japan's largest island, is where most of the population lives. At its mountainous center lie the Japanese Alps, including Mount Fuji at 12,388 feet (3,776 meters). Honshu is home to many of Japan's historical palaces and temples. Tokyo, Japan's capital city, lies on the banks of the Sumida River, near Tokyo Bay in the southeast. This bustling city and its suburbs have a population of 13.5 million people!

Mount Fuji, on Honshu Island, is an extinct volcano. The last time it erupted was in 1707.

Hokkaido Island

The island of Hokkaido lies north of Honshu. Hokkaido has large areas of wilderness with volcanic mountains, rivers, forests, crater lakes, and natural hot springs. People visit its many national parks in springtime and summer. In the winter, skiing is very popular.

Kurushima-Kaiky Bridge connects the small island of Oshima to Shikoku Island. The world's longest suspension bridge, it was opened in 1999.

Shikoku Island

Shikoku is the smallest of Japan's four main islands. It is separated from Honshu by the Seto Inland Sea. The Inland Sea has 3,000 tiny islands, many of which are connected by long bridges! Shikoku is famous for a pilgrimage route with 88 temples followed by Shingon Buddhists.

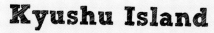

Kyushu Island

Kyushu in the south has a mild climate with lush, green countryside, hot springs, and volcanic mountains. Some of the Unzen volcanoes in the Nagasaki Prefecture (district) on the west coast produce hot gas and flowing lava at times. The city of Nagasaki is a port in the southwest of the island. The United States dropped an atomic bomb that destroyed the city during World War II (1939–1945). Nagasaki has since been rebuilt.

DID YOU KNOW?

On March 11, 2011, the Great Tohoku Earthquake caused major damage on land and a series of tsunamis (high sea waves) that destroyed many coastal areas. A power plant was also hit, causing a nuclear accident. Around 19,000 people were killed.

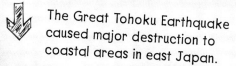

The Great Tohoku Earthquake caused major destruction to coastal areas in east Japan.

Ring of Fire

The islands of Japan are located in an area known as the Ring of Fire. This is a 25,000-mile (40,000 kilometer) horseshoe-shaped line, along which many earthquakes and volcanoes occur. Tectonic plates (large plates that make up Earth's crust) move underground along the Ring of Fire, causing volcanos and earthquakes. Japan has around 10 percent of all the world's active volcanoes, and houses and other buildings are designed to be as strong and as earthquake-resistant as possible.

Food and Farming

Because it's so mountainous, only small areas of the Japanese countryside can be farmed, but farmers make the most of the available land.

Northern Farms

Hokkaido is an important island for growing Japanese food crops. These include wheat, potatoes, sugar beets, onions, pumpkins, carrots, corn, asparagus, adzuki beans, and kidney beans. Buckwheat grown here is milled into flour to make Japan's world-famous soba noodles. Animals are reared for milk and other dairy products, as well as beef, pork, and mutton. Hokkaido is also famous for its fish and seafood—the island produces more than 80 percent of Japan's salmon and scallops. Most of Japan's kelp, a seaweed eaten as a food and used in medicines, is collected here.

Many vegetable, legume, and cereal crops grow well in Hokkaido's fertile valleys.

Rice terraces spread across the slopes of the foothills on the island of Honshu.

Honshu Foods

The Tohoku region of Honshu is one of Japan's top rice-growing areas. Farmers grow rice in wet, muddy fields called paddies. Honshu is also known for its large tea plantations, where most of Japan's green tea supply is grown and produced. Many kinds of fruit are grown on the island, too. Yamagata, in the north, produces around 70 percent of Japan's cherries, and the nearby Aomori district is famous for apples. Soybeans are also grown on Honshu, but Japan produces only a small fraction of the soybeans it uses. The rest have to be imported from other countries.

DID YOU KNOW?

Although rice is a staple food, the basis of the Japanese diet is fish. It is said that the average person eats more than 150 pounds (68 kilograms) per year. That's about a half pound (0.2 kilograms) per day!

Soybeans are used to make tofu, miso, and soy milk. Soy products are staple foods in the Japanese diet.

Southern Crops

Kyushu, the southernmost of the four main Japanese islands, has hot, humid summers and mild winters. This climate is good for growing many crops. Farmers grow rice, sweet potatoes, soybeans, and tea. Just to the north on the island of Shikoku, farming is centered around the fertile plains near the coastlines. Major crops grown here include rice, barley, wheat, and mandarin oranges. The area is known for its delicious dishes made with udon (thick wheat pasta noodles).

DID YOU KNOW?

After Monaco, Japan has the second-highest life expectancy rate in the world, at 85 years. Scientists think the secret of Japanese longevity is eating a healthy diet with plenty of soy, vegetables, and fish.

The Nipponbashi Kuromon Market in Osaka is bursting with colorful fruit. Markets sell fresh, local produce all across Japan.

Cattle Roundup

Although Japan is known for its seafood, people eat beef as well. Most beef cattle are farmed in the west of Honshu Island. World-famous Kobe beef is produced from black Wagyu cattle, which originally came from the port of Kobe. Honshu farmers also keep dairy cows to supply milk and dairy foods to big cities. Pork is another popular meat, so pigs are raised all over Japan.

 Shorthorn cattle graze on the fertile green grass around a pond on Honshu Island.

Fishy Catch

With almost 18,500 miles (29,750 kilometers) of coastline, it's not surprising that Japan is the largest fishing nation in the world. Its people also eat more fish than in any other country—7.5 billion tons a year! Local fishermen catch fish from shallow waters along the coastlines, and trawler boats net fish from the deep sea. Catches include herring, cod, halibut, salmon, pollack, mackerel, crab, sea urchin, and squid. But overfishing is becoming a big problem in Japan's waters, since supplies can run low.

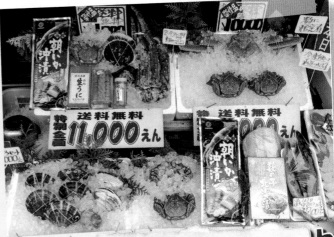

This market in Hakodate, a city on Hokkaido, sells fresh seafood, such as crab, sea urchin, and clams.

Let's Start Cooking

One thing's for sure—cooking is a lot of fun! In this book, you will learn about different ingredients, which tastes go together, and new cooking methods. Some recipes have steps that you'll need help with, so you can ask a parent or another adult. When your delicious meal is ready, you can serve it to family and friends.

This line tells you how many people the meal will feed.

Serves 4-6

In this box, you find out which ingredients you need for your meal.

Before you begin, check that you have everything you need. Get all the ingredients ready before you start cooking.

YOU WILL NEED

- ✓ 5 ounces milk chocolate or semisweet chocolate (or half of each)
- ✓ 2 large eggs
- ✓ 2 tablespoons confectioner's sugar

WARNING!

When to Get Help

Most cooking involves chopping ingredients and heating them in some way, whether it's frying, boiling, or baking. Be careful as you cook—and make sure your adult kitchen assistant is around to help!

TOP TIP

You can choose any chocolate you like.

Top Tip gives you more information about the recipe or the ingredients.

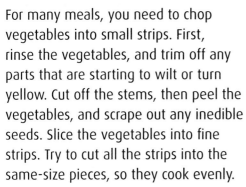

For many meals, you need to chop vegetables into small strips. First, rinse the vegetables, and trim off any parts that are starting to wilt or turn yellow. Cut off the stems, then peel the vegetables, and scrape out any inedible seeds. Slice the vegetables into fine strips. Try to cut all the strips into the same-size pieces, so they cook evenly.

Nori and other seaweeds are part of many Japanese dishes. Add seaweed to a saucepan of boiling water, and let it simmer for about 2 minutes. Take the seaweed out of the pan, and drain. When it is cool, cut it into the shape you need with scissors. You can also cut or crumble it into small pieces, and add it to soups and dishes as a garnish.

METRIC CONVERSIONS

Oven Temperature		Liquid		Sugar	
°F	°C	Cups	Milliliters	Cups	Grams
275	140	¼	60	¼	50
300	150	½	120	½	100
325	170	¾	180	¾	150
350	180	1	240	1	200
375	190				
400	200	**Weight**		**Flour**	
425	220	Ounces	Grams	Cups	Grams
450	230	1	30	¼	30
475	240	2	60	½	60
		3	85	¾	90
		4	115	1	120
		5	140		
		6	175		
		7	200		
		8	225		

Vegetarian Sushi

Makes 10 pieces of sushi

Delicious sushi is perfect for a light lunch or dinner. Most sushi recipes include raw fish, but this is a nutritious vegetarian version.

YOU WILL NEED

- 1 1/3 cups short- or medium-grain rice
- 1 small piece of dried nori seaweed
- 3 tablespoons rice vinegar (or mild cider vinegar)
- 2 teaspoons sugar
- 1/2 teaspoon salt

FOR THE FILLING AND CASES:

- 2 eggs
- 1 tablespoon soy sauce
- 1 teaspoon oil
- 1/4 cucumber
- 1 carrot
- 1/4 white daikon radish
- a few curly endive lettuce or sorrel leaves
- 10 sheets roasted nori seaweed
- 2–3 teaspoons wasabi paste

1 Put the rice in a saucepan, and add 2¾ cups water and the small piece of nori. Bring the rice to a boil over low heat, and simmer for 2 minutes.

2 Lift the nori out with a fork and discard. Cover the saucepan, and turn the heat down very low. Simmer the rice for about 20 minutes, stirring from time to time. Turn off the heat, and remove the lid. Cover the saucepan with a clean dishcloth, and replace the lid. Leave to stand for 10 minutes.

3 In the meantime, heat the vinegar in a small saucepan, and add the sugar and salt. Stir until both have dissolved. Put the rice in a bowl, and stir in the vinegar mixture. Let the rice cool until you can touch it. Put a clean, damp dishcloth over the bowl.

4 Crack the eggs into a bowl, add 1 tablespoon soy sauce, and mix with a fork. Heat the oil in a nonstick skillet. Add the egg mixture, and fry on both sides. Remove the omelet, let it cool, and cut it into strips.

5 Rinse and trim the cucumber, carrot, and daikon. Cut them into slices and then into thin strips. Put the carrot strips into boiling water and cook for 2 minutes, so that they are still crunchy. Drain. Wash the lettuce or sorrel leaves, pat dry, and tear them into small pieces. Cut the roasted nori sheets into quarters.

6 Hold a sheet of nori in your hand. Spoon in 1 teaspoon sushi rice, some salad leaves, and omelet and vegetable strips. Dab a tiny bit of wasabi paste on top. Roll up the nori sheet to form a cone, and repeat with all 10 nori sheets. Serve with a small bowl of soy sauce.

Fried Tofu

Serves 4

Tofu is a curd made from protein-rich soybeans. It is an ingredient in many Japanese dishes. This recipe uses sesame seeds for added crunch.

YOU WILL NEED

- ✓ 1 pound 2 ounces tofu
- ✓ 4 tablespoons flour
- ✓ 2 eggs
- ✓ 3/4 cup sesame seeds
- ✓ 6 tablespoons oil
- ✓ fresh parsley sprigs, to garnish

FOR THE SAUCE:
- ✓ 1/2 cup soy sauce
- ✓ 6 tablespoons rice vinegar
- ✓ 1 teaspoon ground pepper
- ✓ a pinch of chile powder
- ✓ 2 teaspoons sugar

1 Slice the tofu into ½-inch (1 cm) slices. Cut the slices into strips, about 1 inch by 2 inches (2.5 cm x 5 cm).

2 Put the flour in a deep plate. Crack the eggs onto a second plate, and whisk them with a fork. Sprinkle the sesame seeds across a third plate.

DID YOU KNOW?

Tofu has very little flavor of its own, but it absorbs the flavor of the other ingredients in the same dish or sauce. Tofu is a good substitute for meat.

3 Coat the tofu slices in the flour, then in the egg. Finally, turn them in the sesame seeds, so that the tofu is covered on both sides. Mix all the sauce ingredients together in a small bowl.

4 Heat the oil in a wide skillet until it is hot but has not started to smoke. Carefully add the tofu strips, and fry them for 2–3 minutes. Turn them with a wooden spatula, and fry the other side for 2–3 minutes. Garnish the tofu with the fresh parsley sprigs, and serve with a bowl of sauce.

Sashimi

Serves 4

Sashimi means "raw seafood" in Japanese. As long as it is high quality and very fresh, fish is safe to eat raw! This dish calls for raw tuna.

YOU WILL NEED

- ✓ 1 small carrot
- ✓ 1 small piece of radish (about 2 inches)
- ✓ 1 small piece of cucumber (about 2 inches)
- ✓ 1 small lemon
- ✓ some cilantro leaves, or shredded lettuce
- ✓ 1 pound very fresh tuna steak or fillet
- ✓ 4 teaspoons wasabi paste
- ✓ 10 tablespoons soy sauce

1 Peel the carrot, radish, and cucumber. Trim the ends. Scrape out and discard the cucumber seeds. Cut the vegetables into thin, finger-long strips. Scrub the lemon under hot water, and pat it dry. Cut it with its zest into thin slices. Wash the cilantro, and pat it dry.

SAFETY TIP

Ask your adult assistant to help you check that the fish you are using is very fresh. If it is not fresh enough, it may make you sick.

3 In a cup or small bowl, stir the wasabi paste into the soy sauce. Pour the mixture into four small bowls. Arrange all the other ingredients decoratively on a serving platter.

4 To eat the sashimi, hold a slice of the fish with your chopsticks, dip it into the spiced soy sauce, and enjoy.

2 Wash the tuna steak under cold, running water. Pat dry with paper towels. Cut the fish across the fibers into ¼-inch-thick slices.

TOP TIP

Here is how to tell if your tuna fillet or steak is fresh. It should have: • firm flesh • a clear and even color (white or red) • a moist look • a fresh smell.

Let's Cook!

National Festivals

Japan has many national festivals. The country's main religions, Shinto and Buddhism, offer up colorful rituals, holidays, and celebrations.

Colorful streamers with written wishes are tied to a tree as part of the Star Festival.

Happy New Year

In Japan, New Year's Day is the most important religious festival of the year. The celebration begins the evening before, when people eat soba noodles, which symbolize long life. At midnight, Buddhist temples ring their bells 108 times to symbolize 108 sins that humans may commit. People try to stay up all night to watch the sunrise on January 1, which is said to bring good luck for the entire year ahead! During the first two weeks of January, there are many meals and gatherings of family and friends. People visit temples and buy good luck amulets called *omamori*. These are little paper or cloth tags with a small prayer to bring luck in situations such as school exams or marriage.

A group of friends dressed in traditional Japanese kimonos during New Year's week at the Senso-ji Temple, in Tokyo.

Star Festival

The Star Festival, or Tanabata Mitsuri, is based on an old Chinese legend about two lovers who can only meet one day a year, on the seventh day of the seventh month. That day is July 7, when the stars Vega and Altair cross paths in the Milky Way. People write poems and wishes on colored paper streamers and hang them on a bamboo "wish tree." The day after the festival, the decorations are burned or sent to float downriver. There are many other regional Tanabata customs.

DID YOU KNOW?

The arrival of the first sakura, or cherry blossom, marks the end of the long winter in Japan. Parks with sakura trees are packed with people celebrating together.

A girl throws soybeans as part of the Setsubun Matsuri (Festival), which is held in February.

Bean Throwing!

In February, Setsubun, the start of spring, is marked with *mame-maki*, a bean-throwing ritual. People fill boxes with soybeans and throw them out the window, to cast out bad luck. It is believed that this clears the way for good things to come into people's lives. Everyone then eats the same number of soybeans as their age!

Children holding
Japanese fans
celebrate Children's
Day (Kodomo no Hi)
in Hiroshima.

Golden Week

One of the busiest holidays in Japan is Golden Week, which
includes four national holidays. On April 29, Showa Day celebrates
the birthday of Emperor Hirohito, or Showa, who ruled Japan during
World War II (1939–1945). Constitution Memorial Day (May 3)
remembers the day in 1947 when Japan's modern constitution came
into effect. May 4 is Greenery Day, when people give thanks for the
beauty of nature. The final holiday is Children's Day, formerly called
Boys' Festival, on May 5, when parents pray for the happiness and
success of their children. They hang carp-shaped streamers and
display samurai dolls to represent power and strength in life.

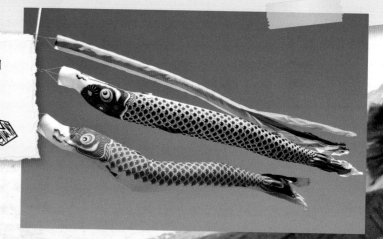

Carp streamers called
Koinobori fly during
the Children's Day
festival in Japan.

Returning Souls

The Obon Festival, or Festival of the Dead, takes place in July or August. According to the Buddhist religion, the souls of dead ancestors come back to visit loved ones. People remember family and friends who have died. They gather at their graves, cleaning and decorating them. They also light lanterns and perform a dance called Bon Odori.

During the Obon Festival in August, thousands of lanterns are lit in Nara, Honshu, to honor ancestors.

This Hina doll is dressed in court clothes for display during the Doll Fesival.

DID YOU KNOW?

At the end of the Obon Festival, paper lanterns are lit and sent to float down a river. These are said to guide spirits back to the land of the dead.

Doll Festival

Held on March 3, the Doll Festival, or Hina Matsuri, is a day when young girls are honored. Mothers and fathers pray that their daughters will have happy and healthy lives. Each family sets up a display of dolls, which are usually heirlooms. The dolls are dressed in beautiful court clothes from Japan's Heian period (794-1185). The custom is said to originate in an ancient ritual where people wrote about their bad luck on the backs of paper dolls and sent them floating downriver!

Soba Noodle Soup

Serves 4

Long noodles are a symbol of long life! They are often served at celebrations for older people, to wish them many more years of health.

YOU WILL NEED

- 2 eggs
- 2 handfuls baby spinach or other tender leaf vegetables
- 1 small carrot
- 2 scallions
- 1 sheet nori seaweed
- 1 pound soba noodles
- 2½ pints dashi stock
- light soy sauce, for flavoring

1 Pierce each egg once with a needle. Boil a saucepan of water, and add the eggs. Hard-boil them for 8 minutes. Drain the pan and fill with cold water. Let the eggs cool down, then drain, peel, and slice the eggs.

DID YOU KNOW?

Soba noodles are very long and thin. They are made from buckwheat flour, ground from the seeds of a grass.

2 Rinse the spinach, throwing away any wilted leaves. Slice the spinach into strips. Peel the carrot, and cut it into very thin slices. Rinse and trim the scallions, then cut them into thin, slanted rings. Slice the nori seaweed into long, thin strips.

3 Bring plenty of water to a boil in a large saucepan. Add the soba noodles and cook for about 5 minutes.

4 In another saucepan, heat the dashi. Add the vegetables, and cook for about 2 minutes. Add a little soy sauce to the dashi. Drain the noodles in a colander, and put them in four soup bowls.

5 Ladle the soup over the noodles. Add the egg slices and nori strips, and serve.

Tamagoyaki

Serves 4

Served hot from stalls, these yummy rolled omelets are a popular festival food. They are also delicious cold, so they are ideal for lunch boxes!

YOU WILL NEED

- ✔ 8 eggs
- ✔ 5 tablespoons dashi (or chicken broth)
- ✔ 2 teaspoons sugar
- ✔ 4 teaspoons soy sauce
- ✔ 3 tablespoons green parts of scallions, finely chopped
- ✔ a little oil for frying
- ✔ salad leaves, to garnish

TOP TIP

In Japan, a deep, square frying pan is used to make tamagoyaki. It makes it easier to shape the omelet into a long, regular roll.

1 Crack the eggs into a bowl, and mix them together with a fork. Add the dashi, sugar, soy sauce, and the scallion pieces, stirring constantly.

2 In a deep omelet pan, heat a little oil very slowly. Keep the heat really low, so that the sugar in the mix does not make the omelet burn when you fry it.

3 Spoon one ladle of the egg mixture into the pan. Swirl the pan around gently, so that the bottom of the pan gets covered with egg mixture.

4 When the egg has set, carefully roll up the omelet from one side toward the middle. Leave it in the pan.

5 Add some more oil to the pan, and then add more egg mixture. Tip the pan so that the uncooked mix slips under the finished omelet, and fry until it is almost, but not completely, set.

6 Using wooden spatulas, carefully roll the second omelet up around the first one, so that it becomes a thicker roll.

7 Keep frying more omelet layers and rolling them around the cooked ones until all the egg is used up. Remove the tamagoyaki from the pan. Place it on a bamboo roll or a clean dishcloth, and flatten it slightly. When it has cooled down, slice it into 1-inch (2.5 cm) slices, garnish with salad leaves, and serve.

Let's Cook!

Celebrating at Home

Japanese people celebrate many family occasions, events, and holidays. Some birthdays are considered to be particularly important stages in a person's life.

Coming of Age Day

In Japan, young people officially become adults when they are 20 years old. The Coming of Age Day, or *Seijin hi*, is celebrated on the second Monday in January by everyone who has turned 20 in the past year. This age is the turning point in life when a young person takes on adult rights and responsibilities. Young men wear kimonos or suits, and young women wear special formal kimonos called *furisode*.

Young Japanese women dressed in kimonos pose for pictures at a shrine in Nagoya, Honshu, to celebrate Coming of Age Day.

28

Girls wear traditional kimonos to celebrate their age at the Seven-Five-Three Festival.

Seven-Five-Three Festival

A child's third, fifth, and seventh birthdays are important in Japan. On November 15, the Seven-Five-Three Festival, or *Shichi-Go-San*, takes place. Parents take their sons between three and five years old, and their daughters between three and seven years old, to a local Shinto shrine. They pray that their children will stay healthy and live a long time. Children dress in their best clothes. Traditional outfits include silk kimonos with matching sandals or slippers for girls, and *haori* jackets and *hakama* pants for boys. Parents buy sticks of *Chitose-ame* ("long-life" candy) for their children. The candy bags are decorated with cranes and turtles—symbols of a long life!

DID YOU KNOW?

During Japan's Edo period (1603-1867), the coming of age ceremony was held for girls when they were 13 and boys when they turned 15. Boys had a lock of hair cut off, and girls' teeth were dyed black!

A boy celebrates the Seven-Five-Three Festival wearing traditional Japanese clothes.

Tea Ceremony

The Japanese tea ceremony, or *chanoyu*, is a ritual for preparing tea that dates back to the 1500s. It has many spiritual elements that are influenced by Buddhism. The ceremony is performed for guests by a host who has studied the ritual for years. Each action is savored, from choosing the matcha (powdered green tea) to pouring and tasting the tea. The ceremony is designed to make people feel quiet and serene.

A Japanese woman dressed in a kimono prepares the tea ceremony in a garden on Shikoku Island.

A boy holds an arrangement of red carnations, ready to give them to his mother.

Mother's Day

On the second Sunday in May, Mother's Day, or *Haha no hi*, honors Japanese mothers everywhere. Children give their mothers special gifts, such as a bouquet of red carnations or a poem or drawing they have made at school. Children help out with housework and cook a meal, or they might take their mother out to lunch. Father's Day, *Chichi no hi*, is celebrated on the third Sunday in June.

Christmas

Along with Shinto and Buddhist festivals, some people also celebrate Christmas, but not as a religious holiday. They set up Christmas trees in their homes, and parents give their children presents. For some Buddhists, a monk named *Hoteiosho* comes instead of Santa Claus to bring the children presents!

A young Japanese family poses for a celebration photograph in front of their Christmas tree.

Wedding Days

Japanese weddings often take place in the springtime or fall. Two people are officially married when they sign a document, but most couples want to have a ceremony anyway. Many weddings follow Shinto traditions. The couple say their marriage vows and drink sake (rice wine). Later, guests join them at a reception. Other couples may choose to have a Christian-style wedding instead.

A newly married couple outside the Itsukushima Shinto Shrine on the island of Miyajima after saying their wedding vows.

Sukiyaki

Serves 4

Traditionally, sukiyaki is made at the table, and people sit and cook their own food. This yummy recipe calls for beef, tofu, noodles, and vegetables.

YOU WILL NEED

- 1 pound 2 ounces beef fillet
- 4 ounces cellophane noodles
- 2 bunches scallions
- 3 large carrots
- 12 ounces fresh shiitake mushrooms
- 9 ounces tofu
- 2/3 cup soy sauce
- 2/3 cup vegetable stock
- 1 tablespoon cooking oil
- 3 teaspoons sugar
- white pepper
- your favorite dipping sauces

1 Put the meat on a cutting board, and slice it into thin slices. Put the noodles in a bowl, and pour boiling water over them. Let them soak for 5 minutes.

2 Rinse and trim the scallions. Cut the white parts into thin, slanted rings. Slice the green parts into 2-inch (5 cm) sticks, and cut them in half lengthwise. Using a clean, damp dishcloth, wipe the mushrooms clean. Cut the mushrooms into thick strips.

3 Drain the tofu, and cut the brick into slices. Drain the cellophane noodles in a colander. Slowly heat the vegetable stock over low heat, and stir in the soy sauce.

4 Heat the cooking oil in a wok. Sprinkle in the sugar, stirring it until it caramelizes. Very carefully add the stock-soy sauce mix to the wok, a little at a time. It will sizzle!

5 Put a slice of meat in the stock, cook it for 5 minutes, then push it to the edge of the wok. Pour in more stock, add some of the sliced vegetables and tofu, and cook for a few minutes. The sauce should just cover the bottom of the skillet. Continue cooking more meat and vegetables, adding a little stock as you go. Using chopsticks, guests pick out what they'd like to eat as you cook! They dip the food in the dipping sauces and eat it with the noodles.

shrimp Tempura

Serves 4

This dish is fun to make and tastes scrumptious!
Pieces of vegetables and shrimp are dipped in
a delicate batter and fried for just a minute each.

YOU WILL NEED

- ✓ 14 ounces broccoli
- ✓ 12 ounces zucchini
- ✓ 12 ounces thin green beans
- ✓ 7 ounces peeled shrimp (with their tails on)
- ✓ 1 cup all-purpose flour
- ✓ 2 egg yolks
- ✓ 1 cup ice-cold water
- ✓ ½ teaspoon salt
- ✓ oil for deep frying

1 Wash and prepare all the vegetables.
Cut the broccoli florets into smaller
pieces. Slice the zucchini, then cut the
slices in half. Chop the ends off the beans,
but leave them whole. Rinse the shrimp
in cold water in a colander.

TOP TIP

Make the perfect light
tempura batter by gently
stirring the ingredients
with chopsticks.

2 Add water to a large saucepan until it is three-quarters full, and boil. Cook one vegetable at a time—the broccoli for 4 minutes, the zucchini for 2 minutes, and the beans for 5 minutes. The vegetables should still be crunchy. Using a slotted spoon, lift the half-cooked vegetables out of the water, and rinse them with cold water. Pat dry with a paper towel.

3 Put all the vegetable pieces and the shrimp in a plastic bag. Add ½ cup of the flour, seal the bag, and shake well to coat everything with flour. Remove the shrimp and vegetables from the bag.

4 When you are ready to eat, make the batter. Mix the egg yolks, the ice-cold water, the other ½ cup flour, and the salt. In a fondue pan, heat the oil and make sure it is really hot before you start cooking.

5 To cook the tempura, hold a shrimp or vegetable piece with a fork or chopsticks, dip it in the batter, and plunge it in the hot oil for 1 minute. The tempura is ready to eat, but it will be very hot, so be careful not to burn your mouth! Repeat for each piece of vegetable and shrimp.

Daily Life in Japan

Around three-quarters of Japanese people live in large cities. The most important city is the capital, Tokyo. People work and study hard to be successful.

City Life

Japan's major cities, such as Tokyo, Osaka, Kyoto, and Kobe, are crowded and very busy. People work in global industries that make products such as cars, hi-fi equipment, cameras, phones, televisions, and robots. Commuters travel to and from work on buses, trains, and subways. They work and study hard, but there are fun things to do, too. People visit museums, historic palaces, amusement parks, and zoos, or they go to gardens and parks to relax.

Shoppers walk through the crowded Takeshita Dori, Toyko's trendy fashion district.

Commuters in a packed subway car in Tokyo. The city has one of the world's largest and most efficient transportation systems.

This large, airy Japanese room has a traditional tatami mat floor covering. It is made from rush-covered straw.

Japanese Homes

In the past, people lived in traditional Japanese houses made from wood. Floors were covered with a tatami, a woven straw mat. Today, even though many people live in Western-style houses or apartments, they usually have one traditional Japanese room. People take their shoes off at the entrance of the home to keep the floors clean.

Life in the Country

In the countryside, life is slower-paced, but people are just as hardworking as those in the cities. Many work on farms or in small businesses in villages and towns, where some people might do two jobs. Rural businesses often run on a barter system, where people exchange goods or food for other goods or food without using money. In remote mountain villages, children walk or take the bus to the nearest school. Life can be hard, and many younger people are moving to big cities. This is hurting communities because there are fewer people to work in traditional rural jobs, such as farming.

Japanese farmers pick lavender by hand. The blossoms are used to make oil and perfumes.

Japanese middle school students work on a chemistry experiment in the school science lab.

School Days

In Japan, children go to elementary school for six years, followed by middle school for three years. After that, they attend high school for three years. Students who want to go to college must take difficult exams, and if they pass, they may attend a university for four years. The school day is divided into classes studying math, science, crafts, gym, social studies, and English. And of course, they study the Japanese language! Written Japanese is difficult to learn: It has around 50,000 *kanji*, or characters. Students must master over 2,000 *kanji* by the end of high school.

DID YOU KNOW?

Japanese children bring a bento, or lunch box, to school. It has different compartments for rice, vegetables, fish, and fruit.

A young Japanese family shares sukiyaki, a meal cooked at the table. Each person picks out what they want to eat from the serving dish.

Time Off

In Japan, time away from long hours at school or work is precious. Children go to after-school clubs for activities such as baseball, music, or art. Martial arts, such as karate, kendo, and aikido, are popular. Sumo wrestling is the national sport of Japan and is avidly followed by fans. People attend traditional kabuki and noh theaters, to hear music and see dance and mime. The Japanese also really appreciate nature. People are aware of the cycles of the moon and the changing seasons, and they have parties to celebrate the first cherry blossoms!

Two girls from a karate club strike a pose at a beach in Kagawa, on the island of Shikoku.

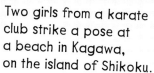

Mealtimes

Because it's such an important food, the Japanese word for "meal" is *gohan*, which means "rice"! Most meals include rice, fish or meat, vegetables, miso soup, and pickled vegetables. Families enjoy sukiyaki, sushi, and tempura, but they may also grab Western-style fast food, such as fried chicken, when they're busy.

miso Soup

Serves 4

In Japan, miso soup is eaten almost every day—for breakfast, after school, or as part of dinner. It is hot and comforting, and the ginger helps digestion.

YOU WILL NEED

- ✔ 5–6 ounces Japanese tofu
- ✔ thin leeks
- ✔ a piece of fresh ginger, about 3/4 inch (2 cm)
- ✔ 3½ cups dashi stock
- ✔ 4 tablespoons miso (soybean paste)

1 Rinse the tofu under cold water, and cut it into 1-inch (2.5 cm) cubes. Rinse the leeks, and remove and discard any wilted leaves. Cut the leeks into thin strips.

2 Using a potato peeler, peel the ginger. Grate it finely into a dish, and squeeze it with your fingers to get the juice out. Discard the ginger pulp.

DID YOU KNOW?

Miso is a soybean paste that is made from fermented soybeans or grains, such as rice. It is used in many Japanese dishes.

3 In a saucepan, bring the dashi stock to a simmer, but do not let it boil. Put the miso paste in a bowl, and stir a little of the hot dashi stock into the miso.

4 Add the miso–stock mixture to the rest of the dashi stock in the pan, a little at a time. Stir in the tofu, leeks, and ginger juice. Ladle into soup bowls, and serve.

MAKE DASHI STOCK

To make your own dashi stock, use 1 cup bonito fish flakes and 1 piece konbu (dried seaweed) 4 inches x 4 inches (10 cm x 10 cm). Put the piece of konbu in a saucepan with 2 pints water, and simmer for 1 minute over medium heat. Using a slotted spoon, remove the konbu just as the water begins to boil. Stir in the bonito flakes and simmer for 1 minute. Remove from the heat and leave for 5 minutes. Strain the dashi stock through a fine mesh strainer.

chicken and Egg Donburi

Serves 4

Donburi is a delicious dish that combines chicken breast and shiitake mushrooms cooked in stock. Like many Japanese dishes, it is served over rice.

YOU WILL NEED

- ✔ pinch of salt
- ✔ 1 1/3 cup short-grain Japanese rice
- ✔ 1 large boneless chicken breast, without the skin
- ✔ 1 cup fresh shiitake mushrooms
- ✔ 1 bunch tender scallions
- ✔ 1 cup strong chicken stock
- ✔ 6 tablespoons light soy sauce
- ✔ 6 eggs

1 Bring a saucepan of lightly salted water to a boil, and add the rice. Simmer for about 15 minutes, then drain. Cover the pan to keep the rice warm.

2 Put the chicken breast on a clean cutting board. Using a sharp knife, carefully cut it into very thin strips.

DID YOU KNOW?

Donburi is the Japanese word for "bowl." Oyako donburi, the chicken and egg topping, means "mother and child donburi." This is because it contains chicken and an egg!

3 Slice any wilted parts off the shiitake mushrooms, and wipe the mushrooms clean with moist paper towels. Rinse and trim the roots off the scallions. Slice the scallions into very thin, slanted rings.

4 Add the stock to a wok, heat, and add the soy sauce, chicken strips, mushrooms, and scallions. Cook everything for about 3 minutes.

5 Crack the eggs into a small bowl and beat them with a fork. Pour the beaten eggs into the wok. Cook over low heat for around 2 minutes, until the egg mix has set.

6 Put a scoop of rice in each bowl. Spoon the chicken and egg donburi on top of the rice and serve.

SAFETY TIP

Always wash your hands with soap and warm water after handling raw chicken. Wash all cutting boards and utensils used to prepare raw chicken, too.

Green Tea Ice Cream

Serves 4–6

This scrumptious ice cream combines rich milk and cream with zesty Japanese green tea. It makes for a refreshing summer treat!

YOU WILL NEED

- ✓ 2 tablespoons matcha green tea powder
- ✓ 1/3 cup hot water
- ✓ 2 egg yolks
- ✓ 3/4 cup milk
- ✓ 2 tablespoons sugar
- ✓ 3/4 cup heavy cream

1 In a large bowl, mix the matcha green tea powder and the hot water. Stir well, then set the bowl to one side.

2 Put the egg yolks in a saucepan with high sides. Using a fork or whisk, beat the egg yolks until they are smooth. Then stir in the milk and sugar.

3 Heat the egg and milk mixture over very low heat. Keep stirring all the time until the mixture thickens.

TOP TIP

People drink different teas at different temperatures in Japan. To make matcha green tea, put 1 teaspoon of powder in a teapot, and add 6 cups hot water at 160°F. Stir well with a bamboo tea whisk.

4 Half-fill a large mixing bowl with ice-cold water and ice cubes. Put the saucepan with the egg mixture into this bowl, and stir in the tea powder mixture. Put the cream in a large measuring cup, and whisk it until it forms stiff peaks.

5 Using a figure-eight motion, gently stir the stiff cream into the egg and tea mixture. When it is well-combined, put it in a container and freeze for at least 3 hours before serving.

Glossary

amulet An object that is said to bring good luck and protection to the person who carries it.

bento A Japanese lunch box with compartments for several different dishes that often include sushi and tamagoyaki.

Buddhism One of the two main Japanese religions. It was founded by Siddartha Gautama in India, in the fifth century BC. Many people follow both Buddhist and Shinto beliefs.

dashi A Japanese broth or stock made from seaweed. It is the base for miso and other soups and sauces.

green tea The most common tea in Japan. It is drunk daily and served during the tea ceremony. It is also used as an ingredient in many dishes.

heirloom A valuable object that has been passed down in a family for several generations.

kimono The traditional silk dress worn by Japanese women. There are many different designs.

miso A food made from fermented soybeans and other ingredients. Miso is an ingredient of miso soup, which is eaten before meals or for breakfast.

omikuji A paper fortune that can be bought at a Shinto temple.

samurai A member of an important military caste in feudal Japan.

Shinto One of the two main Japanese religions. It blends a worship of ancestors and nature spirits with a belief in a sacred power that exists in everything.

soba Long, thin buckwheat noodles. The noodles are a symbol of longevity, or a long life.

sushi A dish made from rice flavored with vinegar, vegetables or seafood, and ginger or wasabi. The outer casing is made from edible nori seaweed.

tamagoyaki A Japanese rolled omelet, made with several layers of cooked egg.

tofu A bean curd made from soybeans. Tofu is an ingredient in many vegetarian dishes in Japan.

Further Resources

Books

Broderick, Setsu.
Japanese Traditions: Rice Cakes, Cherry Blossoms and Matsuri: A Year of Seasonal Japanese Festivities.
Tuttle Publishing, North Clarendon, VT: 2010.

Moore, Willamarie.
All About Japan: Stories, Songs, Crafts and More.
Tuttle Publishing, North Clarendon, VT: 2011.

Otowa, Rebecca.
My Awesome Japan Adventure: A Diary About the Best 4 Months Ever!
Tuttle Publishing, North Clarendon, VT: 2013.

Wagner, Lisa.
Cool World Cooking: Fun and Tasty Recipes for Kids!.
Scarletta Junior Readers, Minneapolis: 2013.

Wiltshire, Diane, and Huey, Jeanne.
Japan for Kids: The Ultimate Guide for Parents and Their Children.
Kodansha International, 2000.

Websites

Due to the changing nature of Internet links, PowerKids Press has developed an online list of websites related to the subject of this book. This site is updated regularly. Please use this link to access the list:

www.powerkidslinks.com/lc/japan

Index